CW00665731

INNER LONDON BUDDHA

MICK GUFFAN

selected & unpublished poems 1999-2006

preface by **Alan Dent**

illustration by **Krent Able**

INNER LONDON

BUDDHA

TANGERINE PRESS • LONDON • 2018

ISBN 978-1-910691-24-3 (paperback)
      978-1-910691-23-6 (hardback)

INNER LONDON BUDDHA. COPYRIGHT © 2018 THE ESTATE OF MICK GUFFAN
PREFACE. COPYRIGHT © 2018 ALAN DENT
ILLUSTRATION. COPYRIGHT © 2018 KRENT ABLE
THIS EDITION FIRST PUBLISHED 2018 BY TANGERINE PRESS
18 RIVERSIDE ROAD
GARRATT BUSINESS PARK
LONDON
SW17 0BA
ENGLAND
eatmytangerine.com
PRINTED IN ENGLAND
ALL RIGHTS RESERVED   ·

Tangerine Press books are printed on acid-free paper

Acknowledgements

Grateful acknowledgement is given to the editors of the following publications, where some of these poems first appeared: *Alligator Stew, Bard, The Black Mountain Review, The Blackheath Counter Cultural Review, Concrete Meat Sheet, Eclipse, Hand Job Zine, International Times, Lateral Moves, Mineshaft, Outlaw, The Penniless Press, The Reater, The Reiver's Stone* (anthology, Ettrick Forest Press, 2010), *Relapse, Rising* and *The Yellow Crane*. Respect and thanks are due to: Alan Dent; Krent Able; John Gladdy for his 'Portrait of William Ogden'; Ruthie Wantling; Jim Burns; Heathcote Williams; Abbie Foxton; Adrian Manning; Salena Godden; James Kelman; Trevor Reeves; Hone Tuwhare; Peter Olds; Richard Goodley; Michael Buckerfield; Jeffrey Weinberg; Tim Wells; John Dorsey; Everett Rand; Chris Wilson; Billy Childish; Steve Lowe; Sophie Polyviou; Benjamin Myers; Adelle Stripe; Lisa Cradduck; Danielle Quinn; Nick Lee; Thurston Moore; Jonny Illingworth; Pete Lally; Edwina Roberts; Jenni Fagan; Joseph Ridgwell; Neal Brown; Lee White; John Sandars; Will Wright; Mirella Sikorski; Dean Harvard; Geraint Hughes; Sophie Cameron and Roger James Guffan (1975-93). Finally, the publisher wishes to extend an extra special thank you to the Guffan Clan for their continued support, patience and understanding.

— MICHAEL CURRAN

Other books by Mick Guffan

Building the Quoins

Little Wars

Spoor Beast

Emoshun iz My Bizness

The Prickish Smell of Unwanted Cum: Love Poems

Inner London Buddha

Twenty Six Letters Scattered Sorted Loved & Unleashed

Cigarette Papers Through a Bottle

The Blahsted Nark★

Mick Guffan is a Bad Vibe★

The Sole of Discreshun★

The Quoin Fellow★

The Master of Fuck All★

★ *unpublished*

Table of Contents

Preface

THESE POEMS COME FROM PLACES YOU DON'T WANT TO BE. Unrhymed, sometimes short, often narratives, composed in a simple style, do they set out to please? They do, by virtue of their clarity, but they alienate too. They are missives from the territories our culture wishes to forget. They tell of loneliness, outsidership, failed, broken love, temporary homes, disturbing (all senses) neighbours, dependence on alcohol and drugs. They might elicit the question: why focus on those who can't find a easy, comfortable place in society when so many can? Yet perhaps such a question would be naïve. Are these poems evocative of a common condition? The voices which speak here (which may be those of a single persona but readily lend themselves to the notion of a multiplicity of testimonies) don't come from those who are viewed as successes; but are they very different from the sensibilities at play in this book? Don't the rich spend heavily on booze and drugs? Isn't there a culture of sexual abuse at the heart of our most seemingly respectable institutions? Don't millions buy lottery tickets every week in the hope they can give up their boring jobs?

What distinguishes the tenor here from that of the official culture is the absence of hypocrisy. The demeaning circumstances aren't concentrated on out of self-pity or a desire to wallow but because there is no escape. Gregor Samsa didn't choose to turn into a giant insect. Nor do the characters who speak here choose their bitter experience. They face it with a direct gaze and try to make some sense of it and to envisage some improvement. Yet when you are at the bottom, either of the social hierarchy or your psyche, it's a long way up and the first step is the hardest.

There is no conscious political ideology at play. These are not poems convinced by parties or programmes. They come from that arena of the lost where voting seems as hopeless as anything else. At times they provoke disgust, at others horror but also pity. They are reminders that the distance between joy and despair is infinitesimally small. Their authenticity is the evocation of the mentality within which their personas are trapped. It isn't pleasant or enviable. It is where most of us don't want to be, but too many of us are.

This is not the kind of poetry which wins prizes, but if it reminds us that what we are supposed to believe about our culture is far from a truthful picture, it may help to turn our thoughts in a better direction.

— ALAN DENT

For a man to have died who might have been wise and was not, this I call a tragedy.

— Jack London

INNER LONDON BUDDHA
SELECTED POEMS 1999–2006

Faking sleep
playing dead–
it was the best way.

MEETING

Your mantelpiece remains
a decoration of no fire
public houses anticipate your
entrance;
resting against a bench
and waiting for the touch on your arm
is the black sun
rising
swapping shadows for
dreams.

TALKING IN BED

It all started with me laughing
at a mystery.
I don't know how it went
from nothing to this:
reading people's fortunes
from plates.
The ones they had eaten from
scraped and scooped with
knives, forks, spoons
wiped down with bread, all that.
And she would tell them.
The mystery was:
what if they licked their plates clean?
That was when I started
to laugh. So I asked her:
Are you a witch?
Sitting bolt upright
alert to an injustice
she stared at me and said:
A bitch? Am I a bitch?
Did you say am I a bitch?
Those mysteries again.
I had laughed.
Now it was her turn.

NO CONDUCTOR

A shame
all this
cos it's a good feeling
despite the hurt.

That uneven balance—
the feeder
the winner
the game.

And my arms
curl, twist and turn
circles and return
again; I am no conductor
a bloodied orchestra
in my heart.

A solo bugle leans in
terrorises and teases—

As Wantling said:
'to be without love is inexcusable'
and then
'to love is the most difficult of all'

Yes, a shame
all this
the hurt
along the way—
to where?

Let's leave it at that.

PLASTIC CIDER TEAT

It's eight o'clock in the morning and
I drive past the empty shops and closed curry houses of
Upper Tooting Road.
A fat, middle-aged man sets himself down on a bench.
I sit in traffic and watch as he produces a two litre
bottle of Strongbow from a carrier bag.
He unscrews the blue cap.
Raised skywards
with closed eyes
his eager mouth pulls on the plastic cider teat
crushing it with a *snap* in the middle.
The golden liquid sloshes and bounces around inside
fizzing up a furious head.
A woman and her little boy walk past him.
For a moment, I forget where I am going.

CIGARETTE PAPERS THROUGH A BOTTLE

Fortune told a lie
today
and I believed it.

It told of money
and ends of the
rainbow.

It said:
There's money to
be made.

I believed it, yes.

So that leaves me
with a fat one
a good mantelpiece
a set down beer
and I can see
cigarette papers
through
a bottle.

A cat in my road
laughs with me.

She knows too.

We are one in
a better
place.

BROOMHANDLE

They walked
in

and there
it was.

They found
it.

She had told
him about it

but he did
not believe
her.

A condom
over the
broomhandle.

I could hear him
sometimes
she said.

He looked
at the broom.

How do
people get
this *low?*
he
said

grinning
at her.

FLY STONED

The fly has been
on the arm
of the chair

a long time

and I have been
watching
him

a long time

He gently preens
those wings

I gently inhale
from a
fat one

My God, he
has been there

a long time

He's freaking
me out

He should be
out there
buzzing

He takes off!

Only a short buzz
it stops
then
a gentle
tap on the
newspaper

disregarded

The fly was
on the arm
of the chair

a long time

I shall
remember that.

THE MAN NEXT DOOR

He did not
trust the
water.

Even boiled.

So he used
the bottled
stuff.

He did not trust
people either.

He never did
a favour for
anyone.

Except me.

He did me a
favour once.

He fucked off
out of
my
life
when he moved to
Penrith.

BETTER THAN BEESWAX

When it was over
she sat up
let it
slowly drip
from her mouth
into the cup of her hand
stared at it tenderly
humming a lullaby
dabbing the milky pool
with a forefinger
then poured it
from palm to palm
until it got less and less
spilled onto the bare floorboards
she wiped it
raising a fine sheen
showing all the grain
better than any beeswax

DAY ONE

It's a fucking mistake
I know that
but, what the fuck?
Filling cracks in the
plaster
with vanilla ice-cream.
Another one over:
Excellent. Listen, leave
your number and if
we need you again
we'll call you.
Great, I say
gather my things
and walk out
awkwardly, my arsehole
sore from weeks of
not washing
load up, get behind the
wheel, relight a cigarette
ring my cancer-ridden
girlfriend, tell her
I got the money
and how I don't think
our luck will hold out
much longer…

DAY TWO

I awaken to find
my heart is broken.
Like no other.
The alarm goes off;
I hit it
hate it.
I do not want to repair
hearts today.

DRUNK & DRIVING

I drive along
back streets.

It is hot.
It is Spring.
It is April.

I hold the steering wheel
at the bottom
both hands.

Elbows on thighs
radio tuned, window down.

I feel a hole in
the moulding of
the wheel.

I check all
the way round
for other holes
but find none.

I cannot stop sweating.

It is Sunday.

I am thinking
of excuses.

12 SHOTS

12 shots of whiskey
circled on the table in front of him.
Each hour noted and he is weighing it up.
At midnight, new year's eve
he knocks them back
regular as clockwork.
He cannot believe his luck.
Ha ha he laughs.
Unsure of others' motives
of this much he is certain:
it is the closed door or exhilaration.

Crushed beercans surround him
nipped at the waist like 1950s poster girls.
Except the one beside him
standing tall.
He rocks it side to side.
Empty.
Ha ha he laughs.
Of course it is.

LIGHTER FLUID CANDLE

I tie a lit cigarette
to some string
and inhale.

The other end of
the string is
tied to my toe.

A yellow tin of
Swan lighter fluid
is my candle tonight.

Still smoking
I get up, hop to the door
close it.

I finish the cigarette
untie it and the toe.

Me and the room.

My friend, I whisper
and a warm
feeling wells
inside me.

I rush to the
toilet and throw it all up.

INNER LONDON BUDDHA

I keep taking this easy route.
Getting drunk
when I should be leaving the house.
No longer wearing clothes, now and again
forced into a kimono.
That's what it reminds me of, anyway.
It is quiet and
despite the cold, I loosen the cloth belt
look down the old line of sour pink and familiar flesh.
My eyes naturally head towards my cock.
Where else would they go?
Ah, we've seen some times together.
This is what you made me.
This is what you see.
I am the Inner London Buddha
and my cock is Zen

A NIGHT IN (ONE)

_____

The performance upstairs came through
loud and clear, drowning my radio…

Well, fuck me Sue
we should all pull
our weight.

Then Sue bounced back:
When do you get up for work, eh?

And the other one said:

I know I don't get up
as early as you, Sue
but the evenings—
you could at least do that.
Give Phil a break
for fuck's sake.

Yes, I thought.
She could do the evenings.
Sue never goes out
and she's in from work before me.

Yeah, you lazy fucking bitch, Sue
do your fucking bit.

Instead of walking your dog
smoking your Mayfairs
gossiping at your front door
listening to your tv too loud.
Yeah, sort it Sue.

Sort your shit out
and pull your fucking weight.

Give Phil and me
a break.

FAMILIAR

I unzip
discover my
cock is
glass.

So delicate
less than a
sixteenth of an inch thick.

It is moulded
perfectly.

I cannot tell
who did this
when it became
glass.

All the veins
are there, all
details correct
as far as I
can see.

She cannot
and I am still
in attendance with
her.

A hand lowers
the familiar walk
downstairs.

One touch of
her finger
and the tissue
thin glass
cock
breaks.

But it does not
hurt.

There is
no blood.

I am free
of this.

At last there is
nothing
to prove.

And I can sleep the
sleep of
kings
from the
centuries.

GLIMPSE IN TRAFFIC

Looked in the rear view mirror
of the car in front.
She's ill, dying
eyes twisted, nose contorted
disgusting but
I catch her in an instant
checking for lipstick on teeth.

ROUGHSLEEPER

I had long hair back then
enough to cover my face.
The Threadneedle Street grate
puked the smallest amount of warm air.
I curled round it prettily
without smothering—
my throat crack-swollen
slowly, I remembered.
Then the kicks came
hard and regular:
early hours camaraderie now long gone.
They all had a go
without saying a word.
I rocked with each hoof in the back.
And while this went on
Superman didn't drop
from the sky
didn't spin and return
to save anyone
from anything.
Faking sleep
playing dead—
it was the best way.

THE WILD BUNCH

There's a scene towards the end—
its nighttime, a campfire between them
a pot of coffee stewing—
where your man Pike says to
Dutch (a lieutenant of sorts)
that after the next job he'll
probably just take the money
and back off.
But Dutch spits out:
Back off to what?

NONE OF IT WORKED

Smoked a fat one.

Made coffee

drank it.

Made another

drank that.

Turned on the radio.

Listened to the laughter
next door.

Went to the shop
bought something.

Came back

sat down

looked around.

Had a shower.

Paid some bills.

Wrote a letter.

None of it worked.

My mind is
laughing at me
the chemicals
spawn something there

the non–scientists
among us
call

love.

A NIGHT IN (TWO)

———————

You know him.
I know you know him.
He has that stall in
Broadway Market.
Sells those t-shirts
the ones with
KILL ANYTHING YOU
DO NOT UNDERSTAND
written on them.
His legs are red, an angry red—
his mother says from wetting the bed
then lying on it, the sodden mattress
for hours, til morning.
The lunatic, crazy.
You know the one.
Sits there, complaining of
a headache, a real fidget.
Doesn't stop.
Shouts at people.
Yeah, him.
Twitching, that's right.
You know the one.
I know you know.
You must do.

CRUMBLING

Closed sign
and
a man
sobbing.

A grown man.

He was inconsolable.

It's the little things.

ENOUGH

Pushing away the night
as a small child
pushes away
the mother's breast.

Like the child
I have had my fill.

A LOVER, IN VICTORY

He took a shower
and now he is gone.

She walks tall
to bed, sleeps with designer glory;

awakens at the usual time

enters the bathroom

adjusts the showerhead
to suit her.

The things he said
once funny
now
empty as a yawn.

The water covers her
his presence
an illusion
a trick.

Stepping out, she
shivers—
the water, her love
euphoria
on hold forever.

ARMCHAIR

_____

They're out again
tonight, she said.
They always go out.
We never go
anywhere!

I went over to
the window
and sure enough
they got into the
taxi

courtesy light on
then out
then off.

I returned to my
armchair.

It was 8.20pm.

Exactly.

CONTRACT

Marking others' cards
like them
we soon forget.

Nodding heads
clicking fingers
clapping hands
we forget.

Side by side
row upon row
fingertips touching shoulders.

Wave upon
wave of
us, sly looks at your neighbour
mouthing the same tunes.

Singing our hearts out
for a plot in the
graveyard.

THE BUILDING GAME

At last I have finished with those cunts.
They knew fuck all about building.
I argued with them
angered, irritated
and annoyed them
cos they argued with
angered, irritated
and annoyed me.
Early starts, long days, shite money
but the gang was good and we helped each other.
No toilet on site
so we pissed in the drains.
We'd head out:
Where you going? they'd say.
For a shit.
Nowhere to clean your hands
so we spat in our palms and wiped off on our trousers.
This despite the foot long rats
running riot all day.
Their sharp and relentless incisors
nibbled at our plastic lunch boxes
and anything else
if it was within reach.
We even saw sick and sluggish rats
lay down tempters and teasers for them.
They were so slow we easily
trapped them under our steel-toes
guillotined them with spades
the blood on our boots mixing with fresh London clay.
You could hear their sad little squeaks
under all the cheering and laughter.
Sometimes I felt a little sorry for the sick ones

preferable as they were
to the cunts we worked for.
But there was no room for such emotion in this place;
it wasn't our business.
This went on for months.
That's how bad it got, we got.

PLASTERED

He drove his little finger
right up his left nostril
to the second knuckle

and as he did so
he stared at me
and slurred:
disgustin
innit

THE BALLOON

It was an ungrateful public
and I, slowly sweating and
waiting for the 44, 77 or 270
when the little boy opened his little brown hand and let it go.
His mother berates—
it's a good show
as that prize balloon pulls itself up and out of the bustle and
into the unknown.
The mother tugs his arm, chastises
she won't have it
but the boy is smarter, eyes fixed on the upcoming bus
whilst the rest of us are lost and watch that
balloon drift off over the buildings into a suddenly blue sky

THE BLAHSTED NARK

Waiting, swaying for the skip man—
he knew he had me
and was none too pleased.
Sick in a pint glass
dimples, old kind.
In front of him too.
I could have kissed him
when he told me to *fuck off*
and gestured with his thumb
in the usual way.
I didn't, cos
I needed that chance
that second chance
like a badger needs a saucer
of my semen.

JUST ONE OF MANY

It's wrong
I know

and I have
no right
to do it

but whenever
I run
my tongue

over a stomach

or bite
an ear

lick a nipple

I am thinking
how many times
has this been done.

How many men
(or women)
have done
exactly the same
moves
as me

hitting all
the spots.

Ah, well
I am just one
of many

kissing, biting
and licking

myself to
the last night
of the universe.

DEBBIE

Whenever anyone mentioned Debbie
you always thought of her plastic-melty face.
Acid attack, car crash, house fire, scolding bath water.
Nobody knew because nobody asked.
She was poisonous though.
Nasty poison through and through.
Now and then hanging around with us boys, half her age
smoking green.
If the little ones didn't know they'd scream, run off
turn around, giggle and point.
What hair she had left
would be plaited in with sad little extensions
that swung gently whenever she turned her head.
The skin glistened in the sunshine
like it was coated with some kind of chemical.
Come to think of it, her teeth weren't too good either—
stupid enamel stumps planted in sore red gums.
Sometimes I'd flick them with my tongue.
The others ripped me apart.
I asked her why she told them; she just shrugged and
that seemed enough.
So we kept this routine going for a few weeks
over the summer holidays.
Hook up in the park, go back to her parents' house
roll fat ones, smoke, blowback and kiss.

I started having nightmares around that time too.
Shadowy figures looming in and I'd struggle
wrestle myself free
from whatever demons they were.
Debbie was a demon, if I looked at her long enough.
It went wrong when she got used to me.

Girls like her needed a fight, you see
couldn't rest until she got it.
She told me once that if a woman hit you
it meant she liked you.
They've been hitting me ever since.

MICK GUFFAN SAYS

All poets are liars, that's true
but cowards most of all

and so are you
for reading this

MORNING HAIKU

at six thirty six
the cuckoo calls a spoor beast
to ruin it all

FOOT FETISH LANDLORD:
SOME SEVENTEEN SYLLABLE COMMENTS

Sleeping tenants' toes
First floor room: touch and tongue flash
Late night snack awaits

Lock Púca's oak door
Chiropody an option
Fingerdrum pillows

Foot fetish landlord
His penis a half-mast flag—
Bathroom incident

Lights out, door creak, peek
Headfizz, lifting crisp bedsheets
Foot in mouth disease

Based on the true story of a notorious Tooting landlord,
eventually arrested for his perverted crimes in 2005.

LITTLE GREEN APPLES

I turn left onto Mitcham Road
and it's good to be leaving.
Traffic gives me the melancholy;
I'm too tired to fight.
Then it's straight down
for about half a mile
a quick left, crossroads, pull
over and stop.
I turn off the engine and look, for the
1000th time, at my house.
I open a cold can of Guinness, wash down their dust.
The front door slowly unlocks itself;
a small hand drops down, ends its far reach.
A blue dress with little green apples runs towards me.
Daddy, you cry
Daddy

STOPPING OVER

Not the most comfortable of places.
The arm stuck into my neck.
I had to wrap my legs round to stay on.
In the early hours, the front door
clicked. I heard whispering.
It was dark, cold, a damp cold.
Their words snaked into the room.
I heard a man, low and menacing:
suck me! suck me! suck me!
The whispering
came towards me. I felt a hand on my chest
the weight getting heavier. I moved.
AAAARRRRGGGHH!
A girl ran out, then the man
his belt buckle clinking in rhythm.
The front door slammed shut.
I do not know about him but
that was the closest I have got to
sex in four years.

TANGERINE PRESSED

Biggest of all where I'm going:
no questions—ah, no questions!
Stumbling off to further lands.
No throwing minnows to the bug-eyed;
no choirs, no whispering, no statements;
no pining, no hints, no language;
no more gripping the edges of every table I meet.
Not where I'm going.
None of it.
Just a few more years yet…
Biggest of all was Wantling telling his wife in hospital, May 2nd
1974 —*When I get out of here, I'm going away.* —*Where are you
going to go, Bill?* —*I don't know, I'm just going away…*
So she left, then half an hour later, a phonecall at work —*He's gone.*

THINKING THE WORST

Bet he drills
holes
in the ceiling.

Bet he
backs a glass
against the
bricks and mortar.

Bet he's in the
cavity—
crawling, sliding
shifting.

Bet he
pisses on the carpet.

Bet he makes
the dog
lick him clean.

Bet he's the same
as me.

WINO

Sitting beside Gilbert in that Kronenhalle booth
the very booth where
James Joyce and his family
took meals and drink…
his portrait above us, I asked:
What was Joyce *really* like?
and Gilbert leaned over
whispered in my ear:
James Joyce was a wino; he'd sip
white wine all day
so elegantly;
but he was usually smashed.
A real wino.

MADE IT

Hooded, we
shake hands
You've made it
he says, then
turns his
shoulder
flicks a hand
and I
follow
him, laughing
laughing.

ATHLETES

I move to hidden
athletes
of events such as:
soul destroying
strength sapping
heart ache
mind games.

All are live and well.

Fucking with steroids.

Fucking with me.

BUTTERCUP MUST DIE

After a year, he looked
too comfortable.

Each day
an adoring
girl would
cuddle him
tickle him
feed him.

His cage was
heated.

Yes, Buttercup the
chipmunk
he must die.

So we got an
air gun
climbed over
the fence.

Buttercup scampered
around his cage.

He knew his time
was up.

I loaded the gun
and we looked at
each other.

My friend opened
the cage door.

Buttercup backed into
a corner.

I aimed and fired.

We saw the girl
go to the cage
later that afternoon.

She approached slowly
the cage door
swinging open.

She ran back
into the house.

Her mother came
out with her
and they both
looked in.

The mother held
her daughter close
and looked around and
up at us.

We jumped back
from the window.

After a short second
I leant forward

and the

mother's eyes
and
my eyes

made four.

COUPONS

Where we used to live
a girl delivered the football coupons
each week.

My mother played
but never won.

My friend and I
liked the
coupons girl.

We dreamt of
raping her. We were
ten years old.

Each day we agreed
to meet at midnight
and wait for her to walk by.

And each night
I woke at midnight
stared at the clock
decided the bed was too warm
and went back to sleep.

If only all
the evil bastards
in the world
felt like that.

LITTLE WARS

Tomorrow's child
learns that
roman candles
only offer brevity.

Their
torn packets
scattered
labels floored
as drunk as the moist morning.

Those men and women
the lighter holders
the night before
not settling for
the ordinary.

Tomorrow's child
stuck at his desk
stares at his teacher—
the night before confuses him;
her laughter
her magic
like the
roman candles
over.

The bell sounds—
the children cheer
to tomorrow's child
like war victims.

I REMEMBER

For Nicolette Fountain

I remember, I do
your long brown hair
now tangled with moist earth
and cruel worms
and the weight of seven years underground.
I remember, I do
the hole you kicked through
your bedroom door
after yet another row with your
strange mother.
I remember, I do
lying on your bed
the slow smoulder of
each kiss upon kiss
two of us lost in the immense mysteries
you an unsweet sixteen but
I was with you.
I remember watching the cat
hop in and out through that hole:
landing/bedroom, bedroom/landing.
It was simple and joyous
and we held each other tight
as if nothing else mattered
but the world and its problems were
just beyond that door.
I remember these things
I do
I promise you I do.

EARLY EVENING, JANUARY

I get up
close the curtains

flick a switch
the artificial light
oddly comforting

6.34pm
dressing gown
on
still a headache
still

ROTTEN LEAVES AND PIGEON BONES

Trumpets roar
at the darkness
the mantelpiece
my stage.

I step up to the hearth
bow and wink.

Well rehearsed, I get down
on one knee. Then two.

Then I begin.

Fingers nudge the lime
mortar, ash.

I get a good hold
feet and knees;
elbows rubbing, buttons
on my spine.

Next door, upstairs—
the tv, the phone
the laughter.

Children did this.

My hands, my knees, my feet
take each twist and turn
through rotten leaves
and pigeon bones.

I am nearly up
and the sun
is there
it must be.

TRAMADOL HAIKUS

Lock the lock of pain
Hollow outside my meaning
Smell the tea-brown piss

Unblinking tram-eyes
Talk and you will savour it
Hallway patients loom

Dropped six this morning
Off to opioidreamland?
Groin stabs and blood loss

Any move shoots sparks!
Next door suicide headdress:
a black bin liner

CRYSTAL METH HAIKUS

Clenched teeth, itchy lips—
  tv is a distraction
Fuck it. Where's the phone?

Light up and sink spit
  Beautiful angels on clouds
Sing songs from within

Slumped, left eye swollen
  Head gone, heart gone, one other
Stupor's chain binds me

Lungs full, rain then sun:
  The top bunk recidivist
locked in a dream cage

HEROIN HAIKUS

Tip, tap on foil—
That funk... beautiful, washed out
then reaching, reaching

Three days in this house
Rape-porn upsets the neighbours
Vapour trails sigh

Sea of burnt silver
Uneaten chocolate bars
The child in me dies

A knock at the door
Fresh friends back from holiday
What the fuck! they scream

GETTING THERE

The can in relief lettering
is this for the blind
I thought
Blind drunk. ha ha.

On the floor a leaflet 10p a day can save a child
from poverty
10p
nothing
but I do nothing about
it feel the letters
in my hand
a third beer
a fourth
some kind of countdown

No child to question it
therefore a child-like acceptance
on my part
not asking
pleading
not begging
heeding
heeding towards the gates
of Hell. ha ha.

I laugh and drink to some
small fortune that
cannot see

BETTER DAY

Amongst the glass he sat.

All bottles
turned upside
down.

Draining last
drops.
upside down
bottles on
upside down
mugs.
on trays.
on the
floor.

Dust covered.

Job—no.
Prospects—plenty.
Drive—no.

Such plight
pity.

Magpie luck
on yesterday's
lunch.

Park sunshine
in last year's March.

In fifteen minutes
dark chocolate will
disturb a
clean gun.

In thirty the bottles will
be emptied.

In sixty the dust will
resettle.

THE QUOTE

_____

I am trying to
remember

a quote

it talked of accepted
boredom

the banal exchange
of standard phrases

accepted boredom

as I sit here and
eat
pizza

pulling
red and yellow
triangles
from a red and yellow
circle

accepted
boredom

I cannot remember
all of it
or who wrote
it

it talked of dissipated

vitality

the opium of the people is
not so much religion
as it is accepted
boredom

I sit here
trying
to remember

TWO CLENCHING COCKROACHES

Two clenching
cockroaches
not bored with life

live opposite me.

She is an average blonde
with an average understanding
of this year's fashions.

He is worse.

He looks evil, but when there is space
he is out, manoeuvring their purple
runabout outside their front door.

Six feet either end.

She goes out
waves with twinkly fingers
through the window
to her faceless ginger
thug.

She returns

the front door mysteriously opens

before she reaches for her

keys.

He really is the worst of the two.

But I catch her looking at me
odd days

as I unload my car

or make solemn trips to the off-licence

checking in with the Beer God.
Me and Him
we have seen too much

to believe the blonde
the ginger or
their purple runabout.

THEORY

I had a friend
who had a
theory that

if he did not
wash his hands
after masturbating
it made him
more attractive to
the opposite sex.

Something to do with
pheromones, triggering
primeval responses
and actions.

He would even
rub his semen into
his hands, like
soap, so convinced
he was of this
theory.

He was a man
easily pleased and
his evenings were
mostly spent alone
masturbating.

WHO NEEDS RAIN IN THE AFTERNOON?

I came straight
away.

And she swallowed it.

I fell in love with
her at that moment.

I refused to kiss
her until she had
brushed her teeth.

Love conquers most
things, but not basic
hygiene.

THE LAST TIME

Afterwards, it seemed daft to be so
close like this, skin against skin;
cold feet searching for warmth
under the bedclothes.

I was on my back
writing on the ceiling—
unwanted cum oozing out of me
the prickish smell
hanging in the air
like a lovesick fruit fly.

I wiped off on an old, stiff handkerchief
which was screwed up in a ball
on the floor.
One of a set of nine in a presentation box
with my initials on the corner.
A Christmas gift.
I had them on rotation.

Looking over at her, gently snoring
I considered the miracle of air
flowing in and out of a body
once young and so full of dreams.
I love you, I whispered
to the back of her head
quietly enough to be sure she did not hear
another lie.

CRIME

She was 24
Polish
a virgin.

Piggy-backed
her to my
place.

She left
3am
still
a virgin.

VISITING TIME

The religious ones
sit around him
surround him.

He's already buried
as they tease
get near it
smile.

I lean over
hold his hand—
soft, with tiny scars.

I have to leave
have to smile too.

CAR CRASH VICTIM

He slurs now
and in pubs
this slurring
ferments
suspicion

Fate haunts him
the what ifs
control is his lover

Pain ever present
the accidental nudges
shoot sparks to
damaged receptors

the learning again of words
the limping
the dark days…

The car crash causers?
Those boys…

Well, they spent some time
under supervision
and their lawyers
out-of-courted;
after 8 years
their mothers still wept
and their fathers leant
over a bible a koran

A good show

No ending

COMMUNION

There he sat
a fat old man
white hair
yellow jumper

feverishly shaping
the cross with his
right hand

blessing me
he said
and I said
thank you

meaning it too

waiting for a mystery
to happen
a MIRACLE

two other men
sat across
from this
priest of sorts

one fearful
one coping

and the yellow jumper

told whoever was listening
do not kiss me

if you do not love me.

NOTHING PERSONAL

Pushing me under.

Lowering down, looking up
and you
pushing me
under.

FRESH START

Do not turn on
the tap and
expect water.

Expect wine
expect love.

Give up smoking.

Eat less.

Lie more.

A GOOD LISTENER

A blow up doll was
being thrown from one
group of drinkers

to another.

The doll had no holes
no mouth like an 'O'.

Nothing.

Must be one for those
that just
want
to talk.

TRUTH

I see a beautiful
woman in
the street

I feel unhappy
and say to
myself:
Jesus Christ...

When I see an
ugly woman
in the street
I feel the same way
and I say the same
thing

but for
different
reasons.

OOH AAH

That's the
only sound
I hear them
make

ooohh
ooh

aah aaah

Both of them.

Is this all they
can manage?

Do they always
communicate this way?

How do they get
by?

I imagine them
in the kitchen

how many ooohs
is it for toast
how many aaahs for
coffee?

Is marmalade
an ooh or an aah?

A whole new
language is being
created
next door.

The world needs
to know.

I already do.
ooh ooh.

WET AIR & EARTHINESS

I had this habit in my twenties, into my thirties too.
On any given day, without telling anyone
I would scour a map
take a train to the countryside
and, once there, walk about the places.
Often they were small villages at ends of the line.
What you might call 'one horse towns'.
I would find a pub towards the end
of the late afternoon and settle in.
I drank heavily and
spoke to no-one
other than the barman or barmaid
about what I wanted to drink next.
When the bell went for last orders, I would
invariably argue with
the same barman or barmaid who had served me all night
and leave on a sour note.
Prowling those quiet village streets
you were soon back in the middle of nowhere.
I would fall asleep in a field
or in someone's front garden.
Once I broke into a car and slept in the back seat.
I could not reason why I acted like this.
One time stood out though
and changed me.
I was somewhere not too far from London
possibly Sussex or Kent.
I had stirred from a field as was my habit
shivering from the cold and alcohol withdrawal.
The more I tried to stop
the worse it got.
So this time that I am talking about

I was making my way along a narrow country lane
getting clues for the train station.
After a mile or two
I heard a sound
behind me.

A car drew level and a man threw open the passenger door.
I climbed in.
After the hello's and where you going's
he started telling me about
these garden shed experiments a friend of his
had been carrying out
on captured wood pigeons.
Sedating them, then drilling tiny pinholes
in their delicate skulls.
His friend was a great believer in trepanning
and was convinced these endeavours would lead to
an army of feathered enlightenment.
For what purpose? I asked.
We fell silent for a long time and carried on down
what felt like the same continuous narrow lane.
I wound down the window and
looked out across the green fields and took in
wet air and the earthiness of horseshit.
Eventually, we pulled up at the station.
I thanked the man and got out.
Hold it, he said, leaning across, offering his hand
as if to shake mine.
I reached out and he pressed something into my palm.
And with that, away he went.
I looked into my hand
to see gold.
It was gold I was sure of it.
I looked down at it
and made a fist.

THE MEAL

Chewing, I could feel
her foot tapping
on mine.

Laughing too much
she was, at silly
things, things
not funny.

Her foot
up and down
my calf.

Her husband watching
eating
swollen smiling.

It was a glass table.

Playing with her hair
mashing her potato
mixing it with gravy.

What was left
of my medium to well done T-Bone
going cold.

The husband raising
his fork again
more for something
to do.

THE MISTAKE

They laughed when they
told me: a mistake.

I laughed too—
even at the age of ten
I understood.

It was harder to do
with the others:
strangers
on tables nearest to us
looked over and laughed.

We were in a restaurant.
It may have been my
birthday or one of my
brothers.

Even before the waitress came over
offering dessert, I had
undone the top button
of my trousers.

I'm full, I told her and
tried to smile but my face ached
and my heart too.

PIROUETTE AND PUNCH

Leaning over, with the short
breaths of a year
old cat

the black hole of a shoe
gawping at you

the night ready to
beat out your senses
with pirouette and
punch.

Days ending like worms

as God's feathers flick
and moan.

Pinch the candle

the peaceful
conflict of sleep.

THE CHARMER

Yeah, I've been known
to laugh a woman
into bed

Problem is, when I
get em there
they're still
laughing

THINGS THAT GO THROUGH QUICKER

———————

Maybe some of this will fire up
your world
as you suck
then spit out
the foul juice of her
open pussy.

Big cough, then drop
it comes, as it
came before when
you tongued and ate
down there
as if
you had missed your dinner.

This is her, now—
look
at her, beside you;
fucks older men
cos Daddy ran away.

WORKERS DREAM OF A BEACH BAR GETAWAY

———————

Again I
am disappointed.

The pavement is a
disappointment.

The opening of a door
is a disappointment.

My hall is a
disappointment.

My kitchen is a
disappointment.

My teeth are a
disappointment.

My trousers disappoint.
My hair.
My legs.

My toaster.

This poem.

All disappoint.

My friends disappoint me
and I disappoint them.

But there
will be workers dreaming
of a beach bar getaway
at a negligent corner
of an impossible town.

Right there they have it
they have comedy
they have everything.

NO GOODNESS

Torn sheets.
Dusty floors.
Unlit fires.

Children crossing roads.
Letters delivered.
Meters read.

Rain.
Wind.
Sun.

Roofs shelter.
Windows shield.
Street lamps flicker.

I look at this raped version with pity.

Cannot believe I am a part.

FORKED ROAD

It was another day
and it was
not a problem.

SLOW SECRETION

Drunk, a woman once said to me:
What's wrong with a father
fucking his daughter?
What's wrong with that?
Who says its wrong?

It must have happened
many times
she said
in the beginning.

And you have to ask that
don't you?

It is difficult—
and yes
requires much effort.

We are what we are:
meat, bone, thoughts and water.

Then you turn away from
those pointless patterns:

listening to your sixty year old neighbour
through shared walls
at a quarter to midnight
Thursday

He's laughing and talking
laughing at talking
animated, yes

and you
pray, pray
he is with
Louise.

LONESOME TRAVELLER

Kerouac on his chair
The wretch that beckons
Him to the toilet bowl
He knows not the last time
She finds him there
His mother cries
And cries over the blubber
Of her big sweating bastard baby
Vain as a shiny turd

NOTHING IS A GAUDY DREAM

The sense
Has hidden
Itself
So
I
Shield myself
Gaudy and
Offset
Onto other stories
Dated and drawn out
Blameless
Yes
Empty too

APERITIF

Stirred again?
Who knows.

Brainwashed?
Maybe.

In love?
Possibly.

Kidding yourself?
Likely.

THE ARCHITECT OF MISADVENTURE

1:1, 1:5
1:10
1:25, 1:50
1:100
1:500
1:1000

No matter what
way you look at it

it looks

hopeless.

SOMETHING SOMEONE TOLD ME

———————

Alc. 5.2% Vol.

Original beer.

Tip the glass
to 45 degrees.

Pour the beer in.

Fine crackling
sounds.

Hot flushes.

Filling.

Filling.

Stop.

Drink.

Put the
glass down.

Sluggish froth
stuck by the sides.

Bubbles rising
in golden slumber.

Some bubbles
move at
different speeds.

Ever notice that?
No, neither have I.

It's something
someone told me.

I keep looking
for it, but it has

not happened yet.

I know it won't
happen, but I still
keep a vigil

every time I pour the
beer in.

Pour the beer in.

SUNDAY MEAL

You don't share any bloody thing as usual

And she dumped some meat and sauce onto my plate

Try it she said and I did

There seemed no point in dumping this onto her plate

So I left it

And her

LESSON LEARNED

It is not a good day up here;
eyes blocked
by old suns, old kings
old wars.

We continue, that
kindness
forgotten and stored
like mussels

til the oldest day of all.

3 MILES TO 1 INCH

One day there was
nothing for me to do
so

I tried to find somewhere
to go on a
map

but everywhere was too far away
so I ended up doing
nothing
except that this nothing
involved
dying of something
incurable
whilst staring at a
book I am finding
unreadable

DIAGNOSIS

I knew someone, a plumber
from those drinking days.
Complained of a bad back one afternoon.
We told him: goes with the territory
don't worry about it, rest up
stretch a bit if you feel like it.

But the pain persisted.
He had trouble shitting—
we laughed when Heather the barmaid told us.
We kept telling him: it's nothing
we get the same, it will pass.

Anyway, he went to see the doctor it got so bad.
Bowel cancer.
Six weeks later he was dead.
Body was riddled, Heather told us.
We used to say: you couldn't take a shit without Heather knowing.
Turns out that was true.

115 DAYS

It's been 115 days
and they know
my weakness.

Running rings round
maddened bedclothes.

All essentials are here:
oranges, bananas, apples
water, phone, keys.

Armpit-stained fingers
pinch my nostrils.
When that fails
I come into a dark sock.

Paper rustles—*torch on*
Silence—*off*
Clawing at the carpet—*on again*
Silence—*off*

By 5 o'clock I am bored.
A grey-blue pushes through the blinds.
Street light yellows fade.
I close my eyes.
The day begins.

DRUNK

Cornered
reaking piss.

Aluminium soldiers
backs to the wall.

The marching drums
have begun.

Thinking of the wire
in that
hot May sun.

Threatening
complacency
with a dirty
fingernail.

CONFESSION

It seems apt that at the
present time
I should get a phone call
from a priest.

I have done too much of the wrong stuff.

Father Michael talks
I bite my lip and tongue.

In addition:
feeling dry, not here, irritable
fake, snapping at people.

I lost five hours just the other day.

Father Michael talks
I bite my lip and tongue.

THE LONG WEEKEND

He opens the
boot
bags in
flask.

She follows
coat over arm
hair behind one
ear
opening the door.

She does not
love him.

MORNING FAVOUR

The pillows—
dull, cold shapes behind me
not set high enough
on the headboard.
And my heart—
an abandoned root vegetable.

The thick of winter
through a window.

Snow settling on rooftops.
Ah, that impossible weight
its so very pure existence.

YOU MADE THESE BEADS

Leaning back from my desk
I look down and watch Millie
feed her two 6 week old kittens.

It's quite a scene.

I feel
my head swell
my breathing
become irregular.

I blink, raise a hand.

Vulnerable, at last.

You made these beads
and the right one
drops
onto
Millie's
fur.

It hovers there
glistening
extravagant
not of this world.

HUNGER TELEGRAM

Nudging each other
we get there
to that point
laugh
clench something beside us
with rivets?

The right thing, the
lonely nights
nudge *us*
now
Yes, it's the right thing

We
look
climb
help each other
forward to the wind
water
nightlights flicking
and we decide
then

HAPPINESS

Somehow
she came
back
with me.

You live
like this?
she
said.

It is very
sad.

We kissed.

You are very
experienced
she said.

She was happy.

And that, by chance
made
me happy.

Two happy
people in
Tooting.

What shit.

FOUR STEPS TO THE WALL

Everyone's out and
she's at it again.

It always begins
with a shriek
some laughter

then

…oooh …oh …oooh

aaah… aah…

Then

AAH AAAH
OOOH OOOH OOHH

I get up
four steps to the wall
lean in and listen hard—
a floorboard
creaks.

Does it give me away?

OOOH…
OOOOOOOOHHH…

No.

I loosen my belt

and see myself clearly:
alone
against a wall
balancing on a
loose floorboard
masturbating
to the love of others.

Oh Mick, you are a genetic farce.

AT MITCHAM JUNCTION I FELL DOWN AND SLEPT

Bus stop, Sunday morning, October 1995.
I fall down next to it.
I take off my shoes
and socks. My jacket
becomes a pillow.
I suck in a long, deep breath
and curl up on my
tarmac mattress.
I cradle my knees, kiss them
and forget all that I need to do.
It is glorious.
Peace is a word with
three vowels and
two consonants
and that was all
the company
I needed.

100 SUNS

She was the
smell of a
flower
I was not
expecting.

The light of
one hundred suns
over
endless fields.

She is away
from me now
but it is the
sadness
that remains.

The sadness
inbetween
I mean.

The light not quite
light
questioning me.

The dreary fingers
of mountains
pulling at me.

All the while
in this state of
aloneness

love's deep shadow
keeps calling
her name

and I cannot be free.

TURNED MIRRORS

I'm wrapped up in dreams.
No, smothered is the word.
Dream-smothered.
Impossible to navigate.
Hostage to this room—
no colour show here.
Turned mirrors, pressed against the wall.
My face stuck on them.

THE FINAL ACT

That's what they
made me do.
Everything.
It's beautiful, they said:
the sunshine
the lush green grass.
First my t-shirt
but that wasn't
enough.
Everything.
Everything!
Shoes, socks
(grass between toes)
jeans, belt buckle
rattling.
They looked down at me:
Keep going
and I did.
Hosed me down.
Filmed it too.
Silent.
There I was again.
And I left the room
to them crying.

Mick Guffan (1953–2006) was born in An Sciobairín, Cork, Ireland, the youngest of five brothers. He came to England at the age of 18, working variously as a taxi driver, airplane cleaner and finally as a carpenter. He died at St. George's Hospital, Tooting, London on 14th June 2006, his body set about by nervous exhaustion following a gun shot wound.

Alan Dent is a poet, critic, short-story writer and novelist. He founded and edited *The Penniless Press* and its successor *MQB*. He has published hundreds of reviews of modern poetry, many of them collected in his book, *Too Much Toothache: The Malaise of Modern Poetry*. He is currently working on a book about Joe Orton: *Entertaining Hypocrites: The Playwriting of Joe Orton*.

Krent Able is a comic artist and illustrator, based in London. Since 2009, his work has appeared in *The Stool Pigeon, The Guardian, NME, Vice* and *Buzzfeed*, and has been exhibited in The Vice Illustration Show, Comics Unmasked, amongst others. His *Big Book of Mischief* was published in 2012 by Knockabout Comics. In 2016 Mr Able co-wrote and starred in *Ink, Cocks & Rock 'N' Roll*, a short film about his life and work, by award-winning film director Matt Harlock.

February 2018

This first edition is published
as a trade paperback; there are 50
numbered copies signed by the prefacer,
illustrator, & publisher, & handbound
in boards by the Tangerine Press,
Tooting, London; numbered copies
also contain additional artwork
by Krent Able.